# I Can Go Camping

## By Edana Eckart

Welcome Books™

Children's Press®
A Division of Scholastic Inc.
New York / Toronto / London / Auckland / Sydney
Mexico City / New Delhi / Hong Kong
Danbury, Connecticut

*Thanks to the Colonial Woods Camping Resort, Upper Black Eddy, PA*

Photo Credits: Cover and all photos by Maura B. McConnell
Contributing Editor: Jennifer Silate
Book Design: Mindy Liu

20337

Library of Congress Cataloging-in-Publication Data

Eckart, Edana.
  I can go camping / by Edana Eckart.
  p. cm. — (Sports)
  Includes index.
  Summary: When a boy goes camping with his family, he shows the reader
  how to have fun setting up camp, cooking over a fire, and sleeping in a
  tent.
  ISBN 0-516-24280-6 (lib. bdg.) — ISBN 0-516-24372-1 (pbk.)
  1. Camping—Juvenile literature. [1. Camping.] I. Title.

GV191.7 .E34 2003
796.94—dc21

                                              2002010385

# Contents

1 Going Camping 4

2 Putting Up the Tent 8

3 A Fire 10

4 New Words 22

5 To Find Out More 23

6 Index 24

7 About the Author 24

My name is Doug.

My parents and I are
going **camping**.

I help my parents **pack** the car.

We are bringing many things with us.

We camp in a **park**.

I help put up the **tent**.

Dad starts a fire.

We will cook our food over the fire.

We need a lot of wood
for the fire.

I find sticks for Dad to burn
in the fire.

Dinner is ready.

We eat at the **picnic table** near our tent.

After dinner, we
**roast marshmallows.**

Marshmallows taste good!

We also sing songs around the fire.

I like to sing.

At the end of the night,
I sleep inside the tent.

My **sleeping bag** is warm.

Camping is fun!

# New Words

**camping** (**kamp**-ing) going to a place where people
  spend a lot of time outdoors
**marshmallows** (**mahrsh**-mal-lohz) soft white candies
  made from sugar, corn syrup, and other things
**pack** (**pak**) to put things in a box, suitcase, car,
  or other container to take with you
**park** (**park**) an area of land with trees, benches, and
  sometimes playgrounds, used for public recreation
**picnic table** (**pik**-nik **tay**-buhl) a table that is used
  for eating outdoors
**roast** (**rohst**) to cook in a hot oven or over an
  open fire
**sleeping bag** (**sleep**-ing **bag**) a padded bag
  in which you sleep, especially when camping
**tent** (**tent**) a small cloth house held up by poles and
  ropes used for sleeping outdoors

# To Find Out More

**Books**
*Camping Out*
by Mercer Mayer
McGraw Hill Consumer Products

*Kids Camp! Activities for the Backyard or Wilderness*
by Laurie Carlson
Chicago Review Press

**Web Site**
**Go Camping America! Kids Pages**
http://www.gocampingamerica.com/kidspages
This Web site has games to play, information about animals,
and safety tips that you can use while camping.

# Index

camping, 4

fire, 10, 12, 18

marshmallows, 16

pack, 6
park, 8
picnic table, 14

roast, 16

sleeping bag, 20

tent, 8, 14, 20

**About the Author**
Edana Eckart has written several children's books. She enjoys bike riding with her family.

**Reading Consultants**
Kris Flynn, Coordinator, Small School District Literacy, The San Diego County Office of Education

Shelly Forys, Certified Reading Recovery Specialist, W.J. Zahnow Elementary School, Waterloo, IL

Sue McAdams, Former President of the North Texas Reading Council of the IRA, and Early Literacy Consultant, Dallas, TX